LAZY LAMA LOOKS AT

The four noble truths

RINGU TULKU RINPOCHE

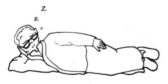

Number 2 in the Lazy Lama series

Bodhicharya
PUBLICATIONS
Awaken the heart by opening the mind

First Published in 1999 by
Bodhicharya Publications
24 Chester Street, Oxford, OX4 1SN, United Kingdom.
www.bodhicharya.org   email: publications@bodhicharya.org

Text © Ringu Tulku

ISBN 978-0-9576398-3-6

Second Edition. 2014.

First transcribed and edited by Cait Collins 1999.

Typesetting & Design by Paul O'Connor at Judo Design, Ireland.

Printed on recycled paper by Imprint Digital, Devon, UK.

Cover Image: ©Getty Images
Internal illustrations: Robin Bath
Lazy Lama logo: Dr Conrad Harvey & Rebecca O'Connor

Editor's Preface

Our aim with the Lazy Lama series of booklets is to publish Buddhist teachings in an easy to read and accessible style and an affordable format. Each booklet is complete in itself, and the series has started out in quite an orderly way: in the first one the Lazy Lama looked at Buddhist Meditation, which is the very practical starting point for many people who are interested in Buddhism; while in this second issue he looks at the Four Noble Truths, which as the topic of the first discourse of the Buddha establishes a foundation and context for subsequent teachings.

This particular booklet began life as a transcript of a talk given by Ringu Tulku in Chichester, England, in May 1998.

Cait Collins
1998

The four noble truths

The first teaching of the Buddha was about the four noble truths. After attaining enlightenment in Bodhgaya, the Buddha went to Banaras. There he met the five ascetics who had been his companions before he went to Bodhgaya, and he gave his first teaching at their request.

It is said that he said, 'There is suffering; there is the cause of suffering; there is the cessation of suffering; and there is the path to the cessation of suffering.' Then he said, 'There is suffering; it has to be understood. There is the cause of suffering, which has to be eliminated. There is the cessation of suffering, which must be achieved. There is the path to the cessation of suffering, which must be practised.' And then he said, again, 'There is suffering; it has to be understood, but there is nothing to understand. There is the cause of suffering, which has to be eliminated, but there is nothing to eliminate. There is the cessation of suffering, which must be attained, but there is nothing to attain. There is the path to the cessation; it must be practised, but there is nothing to practise.'

He said these words three times in these three ways; and that was the first sermon, more or less. It's said that on hearing this teaching one of the five ascetics realised the truth and became what is called an arhat: he attained liberation.

The teaching on the four noble truths is the basis of understanding of all Buddhist teachings and practices; it's the basis of everything. There's no dispute about it; in all the different Buddhist schools and orders, everyone accepts the four noble truths.

Suffering: identifying the problem

The first of the four noble truths is that of suffering. Especially in earlier times, people thought that Buddhists were really serious people; they thought the monasteries must be very gloomy places because Buddhists are always thinking about suffering; because suffering is the first thing they talk about!

Actually it's not exactly like that. It doesn't mean that when we say, 'There is suffering,' we have to think so much about suffering. It's just to identify the problem: suffering is the problem. To understand the nature of this, to have a deeper, direct understanding of the nature of the problem, is the first and most important thing according to Buddhism: if you don't understand the problem then you can't understand how it arises, and if you don't understand how it arises then you won't know how to get rid of it. Nobody, not only no human being but no being, wants to suffer; nobody wants to have pain or problems, so understanding the problem of suffering is the first priority.

Suffering is something everybody wants to get rid of, but what is the real problem here? What is the actual suffering? Of course, if we want something and we don't get it, we suffer; and if we don't want something, and we do get it, we suffer. And then there are many things in our lives which happen and we can't do anything about which also we experience as suffering - sometimes very major suffering. We all get old; we all become sick, one day or another; and we all die. Everything is changing. We can't do anything about these things; and we don't like them: we don't like to get old, and become ugly; we don't want to become sick; we don't want to die. We don't want to have any problems or pain in our life for ourselves or for our loved ones, but we all have to go through them. We can do something about some of them but there are many we can't do anything about. Is there any way to escape this basic human condition, or not? Must we just accept it, or is there a way out? That's the main question.

Cause: our way of perception

The Buddha sought the answer to that question, and the Buddhist teachings have come about as a result of his search. The

Buddha said that he had found the causes of the suffering; and since he had found the causes of the suffering, therefore he had also found the solution to it. That's how he was able to say, 'Now I am free.' Even though he also had to become old and sick, even though he also had to die, still he said, 'I have found a way to become liberated from my sufferings.' What did he mean by this?

This is the main understanding of Buddhism: that if we can somehow change our way of being, our way of perceiving, if we can work on our habitual way of being and perceiving, our habitual tendencies, and go beyond that to see exactly what we really are, exactly the way things are, and then work on that basis, maybe we can overcome the causes of our sufferings.

This is possible because these sufferings come from our own perception, our own experience. Whether I am happy or unhappy, whether I am in a joyful state or in a suffering state, that is my own experience. What is happening when I have an unpleasant experience? I am perceiving the experience as something bad; I don't like it; I have aversion to it. And any experience that I don't like becomes suffering; any experience that I fear becomes suffering.

Therefore the root of all sufferings is aversion and fear; and because of aversion and fear there is also wanting. As long as there is fear, the basic fear, then we always have aversion: 'This is not good, that is not good; this will bring trouble, that will bring trouble.' Because of that we always have to run away from things; and, because of that, we also need to run after things, so there is wanting: 'This is not nice; there must be something which will protect me from this, something which will save me from this.' So I want that.

From this process come what are called the harmful emotions, such as hatred, aggression, attachment, greed, and jealousy. All these come from the two basic things, the fear and aversion, and all are based, according to the Buddha, on an underlying confusion, which is sometimes technically called ignorance. Why do we have fear? Because we don't know exactly who or what we are. We assume, 'This is me, and that is everything other'; and because this is me and that is all other, therefore I must relate to that by either wanting it or not wanting it. If I want it, then I must have it; and if I don't want it I must get away from it or get rid of it.

In a way we are always fighting with everything around us. That's why we have this underlying tension, a kind of compulsion to identify everything as either good for us, or bad for us. Either we like it, or we don't like it; or we don't care, we shut off to it. And all the time we are having to do this then all the harmful emotions - the aversion, attachment, jealousy, pride, all of these - add their influence to this basic tension, leading to our having more and more and stronger and stronger reactions. And the more we indulge in something, the more we become like that, so the more aggressive we are and the more aggressive we feel, the more aggressive and angry we become. The more we indulge in it, the more we become like that; the more we exercise something, whether it's negative or positive, the stronger it becomes; so we develop a pattern. That's what is called karma.

So all our suffering and pain, all the problems of our life are created in this way through the harmful emotions which lead to our reactions, resulting in recurring patterns and habitual tendencies. And the whole process is based on our not seeing clearly the actual way things are and the actual way we are: who or what we are. From the Buddhist point of view, that's the cause of suffering: it lies in our way of perception and our way of reaction. So if - and this is the crucial understanding - if we can somehow change our way of seeing and of reacting in this way, so that we don't have to keep running after or running away from things, if we can be without the fear and the aversion, then we will find peace. Then we will be completely liberated from all the limitations and pain of what is called samsara, the confused, distorted way of seeing and being which brings continuous pain and suffering.

Cessation: freedom from fear

If I don't have any fear, then whatever happens I will have no problem. Just think about it. Suppose I have a certain state of mind in which I don't have any fear, regardless of what's happening: then I have peace. I am not suffering, whatever is happening. If something good comes along, that's very nice, and if something not so good comes along, I can handle it; I don't fear it. So if we can let go of the state of mind which is always in turmoil, always either running away from something or running after something, if we can break free of that pattern, then we get this fearlessness, this liberation, this peace. And that is what is called cessation. So this way of seeing things that is creating these harmful emotions and all these sufferings is based on not clearly seeing the way things are, the way I am, and the way I actually exist in relationship with everything else. Therefore the source of all these problems is basically a misunderstanding, an underlying confusion; and because the basis of the problem is a misunderstanding, it can be changed. The moment our misunderstanding is cleared, the moment we see clearly what it is that we are, or what it is that it all is - the true nature of things, you can call it - then it's said that we become enlightened. We become clear, and then we find that all our fear was unnecessary: there is nothing in us which can be destroyed; there is nothing in us which needs to fear; so what is there to fear? That understanding is liberation, sometimes called enlightenment or realisation because a misunderstanding or a confusion has been removed and we can see clearly now. The way we were seeing things was mistaken, and now it has become clear; nothing has changed, just the way we see it.

This is why the Buddha said, when he was talking about the four noble truths, when he said it for the third time, that 'actually there is nothing to be understood, nothing to be overcome, nothing to attain, nothing to practise.' It's not that there was something and now that has been changed; it is simply that we have transformed our way of seeing, our way of being, so that now we can perceive the way it is, or the way things are; the way it's all interrelated and all interdependent.

But that's not all there is to it. Within this state of cessation, if we can really achieve that, it's not just that I don't need to feel fear and therefore can be free of aversion and attachment, but it's also that a spontaneous compassion arises for others.

When I don't have to worry about myself at all, then the only thing I can do is to think about others' problems, and try to help others. When you don't have to think about yourself then there is no selfishness; so there is complete compassion. Compassion arises naturally when there is wisdom, according to the Buddhist way of thinking.

Path: view, meditation, and action

All Buddhist practice, all Dharma practice, is for the purpose of working to become free of this basic problem of suffering; and it's all based on the possibility of this inner transformation, the transformation of our perception, our view. The Buddha taught that there is a way to attain this realisation, there is a training we can undertake; and this is the fourth noble truth, the path to the cessation of suffering. If we can train ourselves and work on our negative habits, and if we can reflect on and look into the way it is, the way things are, then slowly we'll be able to change our perception, change our way of seeing and our way of being. And thereby maybe nothing changes outside, but if within our mind our perception can be changed then our suffering can be relieved.

The path of training by which this can be done is sometimes described in terms of what is called the eight-fold path; but this can be condensed into three: the discipline, meditation, and view; or, alternatively, the view, meditation, and action. The view is the most important part of it, because, as we've discussed, the real basis of the problem is our mistaken way of perception, our confusion: the view means trying to see things directly and clearly. The sort of 'seeing clearly' we're talking about here doesn't mean acquiring lots of information about things. It means seeing exactly, experientially; seeing what it is that is me, what it is that I am: my true nature, the true nature of my mind. Seeing that clearly: that is the view we are talking about.

It's not enough merely to gain some intellectual understanding of this; we must take it further, into actual experience. There are two ways of knowing: knowing intellectually or theoretically, just in the mind; and knowing experientially or practically, deep from the heart. Knowing intellectually is just gathering information; it doesn't transform us. But if that understanding deepens to the heart level, then it can transform us and we can change: our way of being, of doing, of feeling can change.

This is where meditation comes in: meditation helps us to bring our understanding into the heart, into actual realisation. First we try to stabilise our mind, to calm our mind, in order that it may become clearer. We know that because of our mistaken way of seeing things, and therefore habitual way of reacting, our mind is not under our control: our mind is under the control or influence of the five senses, and also the emotions. For example, if I get angry I will fight with people and think and do and say harmful things, and it will bring me suffering; but somehow I can't help it, I can't stop myself. It's the same with other things: if I feel attracted by something, I have to run after it. My mind is under the control of my emotions and my five senses, not under my own control: that's the habitual tendency, the way I am. So if I would like to bring my own mind under my own control, how to do that? That's why we practise meditation: to work on the mind to calm it, to make it clearer, so that it becomes strong and stabilised enough so that anything that comes up doesn't completely take it over. Through meditation we can learn to see more clearly so that whatever comes up in the mind - thoughts, emotions, all the different things that arise - we can let it come and let it go, without being completely swept away by anything.

The real purpose of meditation is not to have pleasant experiences, or strange experiences. The purpose of it is to have our mind under our own control. If something pleasant comes up in our mind, it's OK, we can let it come and let it go. Or if something not so pleasant comes, like fear, or aversion, or any other disturbing emotion, that also we can allow to come and go. When we gain the confidence that whatever comes up in our mind we will be able to let it come and let it go without being overwhelmed by it, then everything that appears to our mind becomes good. There's nothing bad, because whatever appears, I know I can just let it come and let it go. Sometimes the example is given of an empty house: you can leave the door open, and anyone can come in and go out, because there's nothing to be stolen; there's no need to be afraid because even if a thief comes in he just goes around and then leaves again, so there's no need to worry about it. In the same way, if we can let our emotions and the appearances which come into our minds just come and go, then it's all right. That's one of the main understandings to be gained through meditation. We don't have to be under the control of our emotions and the things arising in our mind. A thought, or an emotion, is transient; it's a momentary thing: it arises and it goes away, arises and goes away. All thoughts, all emotions, are momentary. In this way we begin to see ourselves more clearly. And then we look more deeply, to understand directly the nature of our mind: is there anything else besides that in me? Anything other than these arisings? Seeing this clearly, that's the meditation.

But in order to practise this meditation and begin to transform our view, we need also to work on our habitual tendencies, the habits that we have formed on the basis of our usual confused way of seeing and reacting. We know, not just as a kind of philosophy, but in our actual life, that everything has causes and effects, everything is interdependent. That's the main understanding of Buddhist philosophy: the way that everything comes into being through interdependence. So if we act in a certain way we'll have a certain result. The way we live our life now, the way we conduct ourselves through our body, speech, and mind, will bring about the experiences we shall have in the future. If I'm doing something strongly

19

now, that action will become habitual; it will become a pattern, and that will become what I am. If I'm doing something positive, then that will become more and more my way of being; or if I'm doing something negative, that will become more and more the way I am.

So we can see that the way we act, the way we conduct our life, is also very important; and this is where discipline comes in: the way we do things. If I want to strengthen some quality or skill, I must practise it. If I want to strengthen this particular quality, I practise this; or if I want to strengthen that particular quality I practise that. In the same way, if I want to increase my positive way of being, then I try to create the situations which are conducive for me to do that. And the way I interact with other people, the way I live in society, is by trying to do whatever is positive, meaning that I try to do whatever contributes to the happiness and wellbeing of others. I try to help as much as I can, and, even if I can't help, I try not to harm: that's really the basis of Buddhist morality. It's not that somebody is going to punish us if we make a wrong move; it's just the nature of our own action, which brings about its own corresponding reaction: that's why we have the problems we have. So we have to look at how we conduct our life: that's what is meant by 'discipline'.

So the noble truth of the path can be described in terms of these three: view, meditation, and discipline. And that completes, in a very brief way, our discussion of the four noble truths. We began the discussion with the first of the truths, the truth of suffering, meaning that we have to understand the basic problem we all share: each one of us has pain, trouble, and problems. And even if we don't have a problem right now we have the fear of one coming: 'I don't have any problem now, but this situation which is so enjoyable can't last, and when it ends something else is going to happen'; this fear at least is there, even if there is no actual problem present at the moment. As long as this kind of fear is there we have suffering; maybe it's more subtle, but it's still suffering. So it's very important to understand this, and to do something about it from inside ourselves, not just try to change things externally. It doesn't mean that we don't do anything externally in the world, or in our society; of course we can act to improve things externally. Everything can be changed. From the Buddhist point of view, everything is interdependent: there is nothing which is not caused by many things. Everything has not just one cause but arises from many causes: that's why it's called interdependent; that's how it's subject to change.

But just trying to change things from the outside doesn't totally transform our experience, doesn't totally eliminate the suffering, the fear. There remains always within us a subtler, less obvious quality, like fear, or fear of change, or fear of fear itself, even in the absence of any very obvious problematic suffering. As long as we are in this state of mind which is called the samsaric state, subject to uncontrollably recurring situations of pursuing what we want and running away from what we don't want, there is an element of suffering, pain, or dissatisfaction: there is nobody who is totally satisfied. This inner dissatisfaction has to be cleared if we really want to get rid of all suffering, and that's what the Buddha was talking about. That's what we have to work on. The Buddha said that to get this understanding or this wisdom is the ultimate goal, because everybody wants a complete cessation of all sufferings. There is nobody who doesn't want to be completely peaceful, completely happy; but whatever we do we can't achieve that unless we really transform from within. So it's not enough to be content with just the small pleasures; we have to go further. It doesn't mean that we shouldn't enjoy ourselves; but we should also know that there is a further state of mind, a higher spiritual state, which is the final goal, because until we have that understanding or realisation we are bound to experience suffering. But it's possible to achieve the goal; that's the main understanding from the Buddhist point of view: it's not an unattainable goal.

The Buddha's promise is that, 'Because I have understood it, because I have achieved it, therefore everybody can do it.' That's why he talked about buddha nature, meaning that all sentient beings - not only all human beings but all beings who have sentience, who have consciousness - can attain this understanding or realisation of buddhahood which is the complete freedom from fear, and which is the unlimited wisdom and therefore complete compassion because there is no sense of selfishness. It's possible for everyone; that's the understanding of the Buddha.

In order to achieve it we work on ourselves and train ourselves: that process of training is the Dharma, the path. And it should also be understood that from the Buddhist point of view, the Dharma is not necessarily only the monopoly of Buddhism. The buddhas teach in many ways and by many paths and methods, and they appear to different people in different forms. Anything that's working on our mind, making our mind clearer and increasing our compassion and wisdom, is a right path.

I think that's all I want to say. I would like to spend more time in discussion, rather than just me talking alone and not knowing whether I am making any sense or not! So I would like you to discuss, and to ask me questions, on this topic or on anything that comes to your mind, anything at all to do with what we've been talking about.

Discussion

Questioner: Can you talk about the view? Is this something that changes? I understand now much more clearly from the way you talked about it, that how you see things is the view; so then presumably as your understanding develops, your view changes? Or is there an absolute view that is perhaps the ultimate view, which is really seeing reality? Presumably one's view changes as one's understanding develops? Is that right?

Rinpoche: I suppose so, yes. When we talk about the view, it means we see things as they really are; but it must be that at different stages we see different levels of truth, so therefore we must see it more and more clearly.

Questioner: And so the ultimate view is actually an enlightened view?

Rinpoche: The ultimate view is to see exactly as it is, without any problem or confusion or obscuration or anything added to it. But then, from a Buddhist point of view, seeing it as it is also has many different levels. For example, it's like seeing the moon. If there are clouds but you can see some kind of white light, some rays, and you know that this is the moon, you can say, 'Look, there's the moon.' You've seen the moon - you can't say you haven't seen the moon - but you haven't really seen the moon, you've just seen some light which brightened that part of the clouds. And then you go on: you can see a little bit of the moon in the clouds and you can say, 'Oh, there's the moon.' You've seen a little bit of the moon, but you haven't seen the whole thing. Or there are clouds and among them you can see the moon but it's still not completely visible. Or you see the moon three or four days after the new moon; you can see a part of it, but not the whole moon. And then you can see the full moon in a clear sky. It's like that: the way you see things can become clearer and clearer.

Questioner: So when people normally talk about the view, or when other lamas talk about the view, it sounds much more like an absolute thing, but that isn't necessarily the case?

Rinpoche: If you see the complete view that's an absolute thing; but 'absolute' simply means the truth, the way it is.

Questioner: My question is about samsara. I'm not sure whether it's a cycle of something or a continuity of something. If it's a continuity, if one were to attain higher states, is that within the same continuity of consciousness? Therefore is samsara a continuity and what you're doing is changing it? Or is it like a cycle that you're getting out of? I'm not sure which of the two it is. Or are there cycles within a continuity?

Rinpoche: I think, basically, samsara is the state of mind which is confused, thereby having the potentialities of all these problems and sufferings and harmful emotions and destructive habitual tendencies and the build up of karma. That state of mind is samsara. And then enlightenment is when this confusion is finished; that is enlightenment. Now, usually when you talk about a cycle, it means one thing leading to another. So in the samsaric state there is a samsaric cycle, and if you can break this samsaric cycle then you may get enlightened. When people talk about the samsaric cycle I think usually they're talking about the twelve links of dependent origination: how one link leads to another and another and so on. Actually it's interdependent: it's not necessarily just one leading to another, but depending on this, that happens. It's usually presented in a metaphoric way like a chain, with everything interrelated and all leading one to another; and as long as you have this chain then it goes on and on and you never have an end to it. The chain is circular, so you can go round and round but you can't find the end because it's a circle. As long as we can't break this chain, we continue going round and round, but if we break it, at whatever point, then the chain is broken; and that's enlightenment. From that point of view, that's enlightenment. Regarding our continuum of consciousness, as long as it's in that confused state then we are in the samsaric state, but when its confusion is finished, then we are in the enlightened state. It's the same continuum.

Questioner: Can I ask, in order to meditate, do you have to be centred? At the moment I feel very stressed by the pressures of life. When I try to meditate I'm thinking, 'Oh, I should be doing this; I should be doing that,' and I can't seem to meditate. So I just get up and do the things I'm supposed to do, and I'm doing less and less meditation. What do you advise?

Rinpoche: I think that, especially at the beginning, you must take meditation as a relaxation, as a break in your busy day. You shouldn't take it as more work; you should take it as a break. We are working for twenty four hours, or at least our mind is working twenty four hours, especially if we are stressed. We are always working, unless we are asleep; and even in sleep we are working in our dreams, so we are working all the time. Meditation is a way to have a break, without going to sleep, or without becoming unconscious. Consciously having a rest: that's meditation, if you have to take it like that.

Now, what do you do in meditation? Actually it's not doing: meditation isn't doing, it's not doing! That's clear? So you just relax, and you just be. You just be present, in the present moment. You don't be in the past or in the future. Usually we can't be in the present; we're always either in the past or in the future. Then we're very busy and then we're very stressed. So you relax and just be merely conscious and nothing else: that's meditation. It's not an easy thing to do, because we're not used to it. It should be the easiest thing to do, because it's the most natural thing, just to be present, but it's not easy at all because being natural is not what we're used to. We have to develop it. So you just have to begin. You say, 'I decide that now I'm just relaxed,' and you relax your body and you just let be. Then things will come up: your mind will become busy; it will go everywhere. That's OK; you don't think about it. In the beginning, you have some kind of focus: sometimes you use your breathing, because you can't live without breathing, you are always breathing in and breathing out. So when you are aware that your mind is in Chicago, you just remember you are breathing, you're breathing in or out. That means you have brought it back. It's not that you try to bring your mind back from Chicago via New York and London and through all the traffic and the red lights - that isn't necessary! You just remember you are breathing, and it's there. Then you relax in that. And that's the only thing you do: the only thing you do is that when you are out of the present moment, then you just remember; that's all. And if you are sleeping, it's OK, but that isn't meditation.

Questioner: We've been talking here about internal change, but some people seem to emphasise the importance of external ritual. How important and what is the purpose of Buddhist ritual?

Rinpoche: In Buddhism the most important thing is internal: the mind, working on ourselves. There are many different methods for doing that, including ritual and all the different kinds of practices, such as mantras, and visualisations, and mandalas; they're all used to help in certain ways to work on yourself. But you have to understand the connection between the ritual and the practice, otherwise the ritual is no use. If you understand the connection, then some of these rituals are very important. What we are trying to do is not to work only on the mind; the mind is the most important thing, but we also have to work on the body. The way we see things involves forms, sounds, and thoughts, and all these together comprise our habitual tendencies. So we have to work on all these different levels, and there are certain methods to work from that multi-level point of view.

Questioner: You were talking about changing things in the outside world and also about transforming the view, both being ways to deal with suffering. You said that you need to work on things in the outside world as well. Can you offer some advice on striking a balance between the two?

Rinpoche: Of course, we need to work on things in the outside world. You have to work with other people; and if you feel cold you have to put on the heater, don't you? If you don't fix your heater you'll be too cold to do anything; you'll just be freezing and then you can't do any work on your mind! And also you can't say, 'Oh, I'm just working on my mind so I don't need to earn my living.' When you become too hungry you can't practise. So if there's anything you can do, you do it. If you have a problem like a pain in your stomach you have to take some medicine; it's no good saying, 'I'm just working on my mind and even if I have a problem in my stomach, it's OK.' It's equally important to work on the outside, to care about what's going on, and to see your own and others' problems and try to overcome those problems as much as possible. But I think it's also very important to understand that you can't solve everything only by external means. Even if you have lots of money and material things around you, still it doesn't guarantee your peace and happiness. You can't expect that just because you have this much money or that many friends you'll be completely all right, with no more problems. Your inner transformation and understanding are equally as important. Actually you can't expect to have complete peace of mind and complete happiness without this inner transformation and enlightenment. Therefore you are more or less balanced.

Questioner: If becoming a Buddha means to be beyond suffering, how was it that the Buddha had physical suffering?

Rinpoche: How do you know he suffered?

Questioner: You read about it in the books; you read how when he was older he became ill.

Rinpoche: Buddhists believe that the Buddha is free of physical suffering. His body is made of ordinary flesh, so his body is vulnerable, but he doesn't have suffering from it. It's true that the body is made of the four elements so it has to disintegrate into the four elements; but in the Mahayana way of seeing it the Buddha doesn't have any physical suffering, although sometimes he would demonstrate an apparent physical suffering in order to help people understand the cause and effect of things.

Questioner: It seems that there is in the presentation of the four noble truths a judgement that suffering is to be avoided, but in my experience suffering is or can be a very useful opportunity for learning. It can provide a motivation to learn more about one's life.

Rinpoche: Why do you need to learn more about your life?

Questioner: Well...

Rinpoche: If you didn't have any suffering then you wouldn't need to learn about your life; there'd be no need to learn.

Questioner: Oh.

Rinpoche: OK. You think about it!

Questioner: Could you say that as long as the Buddha still had his physical body he was vulnerable to suffering?

Rinpoche: Maybe; but suffering is an experience, and from the Buddhist point of view, especially from the Mahayana point of view, the Buddha does not suffer because there is no cause for suffering. That's the understanding. If he seemed to show suffering, he was doing it in order to say something, to teach something. But in some Shravakayana sutras they say that the Buddha still has a body which was created by karmic conditions, therefore he might still have pain - but even then, no suffering.

Questioner: How do you deal with negative emotions?

Rinpoche: There are different ways recommended, but I think the most effective one is to be able to look at or rest in that emotion at that very moment. When a certain emotion comes up in you, if you can relax in that emotion, then usually that emotion becomes kind of neutral. It doesn't build up; it can't build up. Every emotion is driven by tension, and if you don't continue the tension, if you just relax in that, the emotion can't be sustained. It doesn't mean that it doesn't come back, but every time it comes back you do the same thing.

Questioner: So in that sense then laughter is quite a good tool, would you say? For example if you're angry about something and you acknowledge that anger and laugh at it?

Rinpoche: You can say that; but what I really meant was not just outside, but from within: relaxing from within. When any emotion comes there is an emotional tension, so if you can you just relax in that, within. When you relax in that tension, then you don't cultivate it. Or you can laugh at it; I think it's the same thing.

Questioner: But when an emotion really takes control of you, what do you do after the event, minute by minute, day by day, whatever?

Rinpoche: It's the same thing I think. The best way, whenever you catch it, is if you can relax into it, so then it dissipates. You don't repress it; it just dissipates. If you can't do that, if the emotion comes up and just comes out and you bang the door, or whatever you do, and then you become aware of it, then you relax. You don't carry it; you don't keep it. I think, whenever you can, at whatever stage, you just do that; that's good enough. Especially with an emotion like hatred, the worst thing is to keep it in your mind; then it's not only harming others but harming yourself the most. So it's no use; so we just relax. And you can apply reasoning also; sometimes reasoning helps: it's no use holding on to this because it's neither good for me nor good for anybody else, so it's better not to keep it, not to try to hold a grudge; to let it go is better for me and better for everybody.

We sometimes think that if somebody does something bad to you and you don't retaliate, then you're not a 'strong man' or 'brave man' or whatever; we have that kind of idea in most of our cultures. So if you can see it more clearly then you see that's not necessary: rather it's the case that the more you keep hold of it, the more you harm yourself. I think that understanding makes it easier.

Questioner: Would you apply the same principle if you're very compassionate and you feel too much emotion because of that attachment to another person or animal? Would you apply the same principle then in order to remove the attachment?

Rinpoche: Attachment is not always bad. Attachment is sometimes good. At our stage compassion is also a little bit mixed with attachment. Love, compassion, concern for others, thinking, 'I want to help everybody; I want to do good things,' is also a kind of attachment; so attachment is not necessarily bad. If you are clinging too much then it brings suffering; that's why it's called bad. But most of the time, attachment is also influenced by fear and aversion; when we look deeper we will find that our attachment is always a kind of escape route for aversion. We think, 'That's very bad, so maybe if I hold on to this, then that which I fear and dislike may not happen,' so we're just clinging for our own sake, falsely. And it doesn't help very much. Most of our attachments are a little bit like that, sometimes when we think we are actually being compassionate. So attachment isn't totally harmful. But hatred is totally harmful. That's why the Buddha always said we should first deal with hatred because that's the worst thing; then attachment, because that's coming from the aversion, which is why it also brings suffering and problems.

Questioner: This is asking for a generalisation, but how much progress do you really think it's possible to make without taking robes, without becoming ordained as a monk or nun?

Rinpoche: Well, I really don't think taking robes changes very much. Of course, you can take robes and also do nothing! You can take the robe and become very lazy - like me! When you take robes, especially in the East, people perceive you as being like a lama: then they give you food and presents, and you can just sit back and become fatter and fatter! So taking robes doesn't necessarily mean too much. But of course, in another way, taking the robes means more commitment; you're committing yourself to it more or less full time, in a way; so maybe there is more opportunity, more time, more interest perhaps. But I think it doesn't necessarily make much difference. The real thing is how much you integrate your life with Dharma practice, and how much you understand it: that's the important thing. From a Buddhist point of view, understanding is a very important part of it. Understanding means not only studies and intellectual knowledge but the basic understanding of how to do the practice. If you don't know how to practise, then how will you do it? You don't know how to! Then when you have that understanding, it depends on how you integrate the practice within yourself. Sometimes you will find more highly attained people among the unordained, lay community than in the ordained community. I don't think it's mentioned anywhere that only monks or nuns can become enlightened and others can't. It's up to the individual person.

Questioner: Is celibacy necessary for serious spiritual practice?

Rinpoche: No, I don't think so. But sex is one of the strongest desires in human beings, so if you can work on that then you can work on any other emotion. The point is to work on your sexual desire, and the practise of celibacy is one way to do that.

Questioner: Why do monks and nuns shave their heads? Does it have any symbolic meaning or does it help in their meditation?

PERMS..? IMPERMS..!

Rinpoche: Shaving the head is said to remove adornment: when you have hair, you want to style it - so it's to stop that! And also to have less work, I think! You just shave your hair and then it's OK. A basic principal of living as a monk or nun is to simplify your life, to have fewer things that must be done; so you just shave your head once a month, and then you don't have to do anything else with it. But nowadays shaving the head is becoming a fashion, so maybe now it's also becoming an object of vanity!

Questioner: Could you say something about women in Buddhism? Particularly women and the apparent discrimination in the Vinaya rules?

Rinpoche: The Vinaya applies particularly to the monkhood, the monks and nuns. It comes from India, and it is a separate kind of discipline which has its own rules, made at the time of the Buddha in India. It's very much to do with the society of that time, so in these Vinaya rules there are many things which are not the same for men and women; the monks and nuns have different rules. The nuns have more rules than the monks: the full monks have 253 things not to do, and the full nuns have 350 not to do! So there's a discrepancy there. In Tibetan Buddhism the Vinaya is taken as a basis but it's not the main practice: the main practice is Mahayana Buddhism, which is the Bodhisattvayana. In the bodhisattva practice the precepts are completely the same for everyone; there is no discrimination at all between men and women. I think it is possibly because there are discrepancies between the rules for monks and nuns in the Vinaya that the full ordination of nuns was never brought to Tibet: they have only the novice nuns ordination there, which is the same as that for novice monks; the rules are the same. So they didn't really observe the bhikshuni order in Tibet, the full nuns ordination. But now, women want to become bhikshuni, and recently many nuns from Samye Ling and other places were ordained in this bhikshuni order. So now they must become subordinate to the monks!

Questioner: Could the Dalai Lama ever be reborn as a woman?

Rinpoche: I don't know. Maybe. In theory it's possible, because from the Buddhist point of view, you can be born anywhere, and as anything: male or female; female can become

49

male; male can become female; humans can become animals; animals can become humans; and beings of all the six realms can be born in any of the others. Bodhisattvas can and should take any form which is beneficial for sentient beings; so if it's beneficial, why shouldn't the Dalai Lama become a woman? He can become a woman, or a white person or a black person; he can become anything.

Questioner: Is it difficult now for reincarnating lamas to be born in Tibet?

Rinpoche: There's no compulsion that a Tibetan lama must be reborn only in Tibet. One of the Dalai Lamas was born in Mongolia, for instance. It's said that they can be born anywhere. The Tibetans know about only those reincarnations who are born in Tibet, but we believe that there are many more outside Tibet, who are not being found, or not being looked for. It's not necessary for them to be recognised; usually they're not recognised. There are supposed to be reincarnations of bodhisattvas everywhere, in all countries, and in all the realms of existence.

Questioner: But what about the Karmapa? Isn't it necessary that he be born in Tibet?

Rinpoche: Not necessarily. This one was found in Tibet, but it's not necessarily the only possibility. It's also said that Karmapa has an emanation in each of all the countless worlds.

Thank you all very much.

All my babbling,
In the name of Dharma
Has been set down faithfully
By my dear students of pure vision.

I pray that at least a fraction of the wisdom
Of those enlightened teachers
Who tirelessly trained me
Shines through this mass of incoherence.

May the sincere efforts of all those
Who have worked tirelessly
Result in spreading the true meaning of Dharma
To all who are inspired to know.

May this help dispel the darkness of ignorance
In the minds of all living beings
And lead them to complete realisation
Free from all fear.

Ringu Tulku

Acknowledgements

We would like to thank the students of the Bodhicharya Buddhist Group in Chichester, England, who hosted the talk and posed the questions in this book.

We also wish to thank the original team that produced the first edition of this book: Jude Tarrant, for design and layout; Robin Bath, for his drawings; Norma Levine, for her advice on editing; Alison de Ledesma, for distribution; and Cait Collins, for transcribing and editing this book.

For this second edition we would like to thank: Paul O'Connor, for this new layout and cover image; Dr Conrad Harvey & Rebecca O'Connor, for the new Lazy Lama logo illustration; Rachel Moffitt, for distribution; and Jonathan Clewley, for proof reading.

About the Author

Ringu Tulku Rinpoche is a Tibetan Buddhist Master of the Kagyu Order. He was trained in all schools of Tibetan Buddhism under many great masters including HH the 16th Gyalwang Karmapa and HH Dilgo Khyentse Rinpoche. He took his formal education at Namgyal Institute of Tibetology, Sikkim and Sampurnananda Sanskrit University, Varanasi, India. He served as Tibetan Textbook Writer and Professor of Tibetan Studies in Sikkim for 25 years.

Since 1990, he has been travelling and teaching Buddhism and meditation in Europe, America, Canada, Australia and Asia. He participates in various interfaith and 'Science and Buddhism' dialogues and is the author of several books on Buddhist topics. These include Path to Buddhahood, Daring Steps, The Ri-me Philosophy of Jamgon Kongtrul the

Great, Confusion Arises as Wisdom, the Lazy Lama series and the Heart Wisdom series, as well as several children's books, available in Tibetan and European languages.

He founded the organisations:
Bodhicharya - see www.bodhicharya.org
and Rigul Trust - see www.rigultrust.org

Other books by Bodhicharya Publications

The Lazy Lama Series:

No. 1 - Buddhist Meditation

No. 2 - The Four Noble Truths

No. 3 - Refuge: Finding a Purpose and a Path

No. 4 - Bodhichitta: Awakening Compassion and Wisdom

No. 5 - Living without Fear and Anger

Heart Wisdom Series:

The Ngöndro: *Foundation Practices of Mahamudra*

From Milk to Yoghurt: *A Recipe for Living and Dying*

Like Dreams and Clouds: *Emptiness and Interdependence; Mahamudra and Dzogchen*

Dealing with Emotions: *Scattering the Clouds*

Journey from Head to Heart: *Along a Buddhist Path*

See: www.bodhicharya.org/publications

Rigul TrusT

Patron: Ringu Tulku Rinpoche

Rigul Trust is a UK charity whose objectives are the relief of poverty and financial hardship, the advancement of education, the advancement of religion, the relief of sickness, the preservation of good health.

Our main project is helping with health and education in Rigul, Tibet, the homeland of Ringu Tulku Rinpoche where his monastery is. We currently fund Dr Chuga, the nurse, the doctor's assistant, the running costs of the health clinic, the teachers, the cooks and the children's education plus two, free, hot meals a day at school.

We also help raise funds for disasters like earthquakes, floods, and help with schools in India and other health and welfare projects. All administration costs are met privately by volunteers.

100% OF ALL DONATIONS GOES TO FUND HEALTH, EDUCATION AND POVERTY RELIEF PROJECTS

Rigul Trust

13 St. Francis Avenue, Southampton, SO18 5QL U.K.

info@rigultrust.org

UK Charity Registration No: 1124076

TO FIND OUT MORE, OR MAKE A DONATION, PLEASE VISIT:

www.rigultrust.org

For an up to date list of books by Ringu Tulku,
please see the Books section at

www.bodhicharya.org

*All proceeds received by Bodhicharya Publications
from the sale of this book go direct to humanitarian
and educational projects because the work involved in
producing this book has been given free of charge.*